ReDesign

Editor
David E. Carter

Book Designer
Suzanna M.W. Brown

Copywriter
Christa Carter

ReDesign - Logo & Letterhead Makeovers

First published 1998 by Hearst Books International
1350 Avenue of the Americas
New York, NY 10019

ISBN: 0688-16474-9

Distributed in the U.S. and Canada by
Watson-Guptill Publications
1515 Broadway
New York, NY 10036
Tel: (800) 451-1741
         (732) 363-4511 in NJ, AK, HI
Fax: (732) 363-0338

ISBN: 0-8230-6817-X

Distributed throughout the rest of the world by
Hearst Books International
1350 Avenue of the Americas
New York, NY 10019
Fax: (212) 261-6795

First Published in Germany by
Nippan
Nippon Shuppan Ilanbai
Deutschland GmbH
D-40549 Dusseldorf
Telephone: (0211) 504 8089
Fax: (0211) 504 9326

ISBN: 3-931884-38-4

©Copyright 1998 by Hearst Books International and
David E. Carter

Printed in Hong Kong by Everbest Printing Company
through Four Colour Imports, Louisville, Kentucky.

Graphic design, like machinery and equipment, wears out. The flashy logo or letterhead of ten years ago may present an outdated (and inaccurate) image of the company today. Slightly refined corporate images or even complete makeovers are necessary from time to time.

ReDesign includes approximately 100 before-and-after projects. Old logos or letterheads are presented along with revised solutions.

This book gives the reader an inside look at real-world projects that are typical for graphic designers. If you design logos or letterheads, this book will be a resource which you will use on a regular basis.

Dave Carter

Ice Sparkling Water had four segmented products, as shown at left. Note that there was essentially a single visual identity, with color variation being the primary distinguishing feature.

The redesign involved the creation of four separate styles, in order to give each product its own identity. One of the new designs is shown below. The others are shown on the following three pages.

Client: **Talking Rain**
Design Firm: **Hornall Anderson Design Works**
                    Seattle, Washington

ICE™

Design

*Re*Design

Phil Rudy Photography had grown tired of the existing stationery look and was in the process of moving to an older area of town. The redesign included introducing the sepia colors of historical photos to the existing colors. The overall effect reflects both the new location and a cutting edge outlook.

209·441·1887

411 e. olive · fresno, ca · 93728

Client: **Phil Rudy Photography**
Design Firm: **Shields Design**
                 Fresno, California

Phil Rudy

Photography

764 P Street • Suite D • Fresno, CA 93721 • 209-441-1887

ReDesign

Omni Media's original logo looked staid and corporate, and lacked any
equity. The updated logo reflects the image of Omni Media as a vitally
creative company full of ideas.

OmniMedia (UK)
North America Division

2390 E. Camelback
Suite 300
Phoenix, Arizona 85016

T 602 912 5731
F 602 912 5732

Client:	**Omni Media**
Design Firm:	**After Hours Creative**
	Phoenix, Arizona

California Center for the Arts' old logo was colorful, but didn't represent the center well. The new logo integrates the initials into a creative, artful logo that works well for the center.

Client: **California Center for the Arts**
Design Firm: **Mires Design**
                 San Diego, California

HOFFMAN ESTATES CHAMBER OF COMMERCE & INDUSTRY

The Hoffman Estates Chamber is among the five largest in Illinois. Rather than using the "HE", the design firm felt eliminating the "E" would be a positive step. Working with the "H" alone, the use of strong, simple, italic strokes with a dynamic, upwards sweeping motion suggested growth and positive business movement within the service area.

Client: **Hoffman Estates Chamber of Commerce and Industry**
Design Firm: **Identity Center**
                        Schaumburg, Illinois

ReDesign

After more than ten years in business, Value Holidays was overdue for a new look. The use of the globe is an appropriate symbol for the client—a travel agency that deals exclusively in international travel packages.

VALUE HOLIDAYS

10224 North Port Washington Road
Mequon, Wisconsin 53092-5755

Telephone: 414-241-6373
Telex: 201323 YWOTUR
Fax: 414-241-6379
Nationwide: 1-800-558-6850

Affiliated Offices: London • Paris • Innsbruck • Rome • Brussels • Shenyang • Dublin • Frankfurt • Auckland • Sydney • Rio de Janeiro

Client: **Value Holidays**
Design Firm: **Becker Design**
Milwaukee, Wisconsin

AFFILIATED OFFICES:
London • Paris • Innsbruck • Rome
Brussels • Shenyang • Dublin • Frankfurt
Auckland • Sydney • Rio de Janerio

VALUE HOLIDAYS

10224 NORTH PORT WASHINGTON ROAD MEQUON, WISCONSIN 53092-5755
PHONE 414.241.6373 TELEX 201.323.YWOTUR FAX 414.241.6379 NATIONWIDE 1.800.558.8850

*Re*Design

Wayne Hospital's past logo and identity were used inconsistently on a variety of materials. The redesign involved slightly updating the logo and maintaining consistent placement of the logo in relation to other elements.

WH Wayne Hospital

835 Sweitzer Street
Greenville, Ohio 45331-1077
513-548-1141 FAX 513-547-5712

WH

Wayne Hospital
835 Sweitzer Street
Greenville, Ohio 45331-1077

Client: **Wayne Hospital**
Design Firm: **1-earth GRAPHICS**
                     Troy, Ohio

WH
WAYNE
HOSPITAL

835 Sweitzer Street · Greenville, Ohio 45331-1077 · 937-548-1141 · Fax 937-547-5712

WH
WAYNE
HOSPITAL

835 Sweitzer Street · Greenville, Ohio 45331-1077

CUBE Advertising/Design chose to create a business card that was more indicative of its name than the original logo. The new card is die cut so that the white and black squares "pop up" into a cube when the card is folded—very memorable.

Client: **CUBE Advertising/Design**
Design Firm: **CUBE Advertising/Design**
St. Louis, Missouri

David Kingsbury Photography's original design worked well design-wise, but lacked originality. In the redesign, CUBE utilizes exciting color and a camera logo to create a stylish business card.

Client: **David Kingsbury Photography**
Design Firm: **CUBE Advertising/Design**
                St. Louis, Missouri

Design

The information explosion has increased the amount of information needed on letterheads. In updating the letterhead to meet this need, AERIAL redesigned the letterhead to reflect R.J. Muna's photography business.

RJ MUNA
PHOTOGRAPHY

RJ MUNA
PHOTOGRAPHY

225 Industrial Street, San Francisco, CA 94124 · 415 · 468 · 8225 PHONE · 415 · 468 · 8295 FAX

Client: **R.J. Muna**
Design Firm: **A E R I A L**
                 San Francisco, California

Design

R J MUNA
PICTURES

R J MUNA
PICTURES

225 INDUSTRIAL STREET
SAN FRANCISCO, CALIFORNIA
ZIP 94124-8975

225 INDUSTRIAL STREET
SAN FRANCISCO, CALIFORNIA
ZIP 94124-8975

TEL 415.468.8225
FAX 415.468.8295
NET pictures@rjmuna.com

Keebler Fudge Shoppe's line had five separate products, as shown below. Although the five products had a single identity, color variation created individual identity. The redesign involved updating the package styles, shown right, keeping the same color variations.

Client: **Keebler Fudge Shoppe**
Design Firm: **Harbauer Bruce Design**
               Chicago, Illinois

ReDesign

Ralph Fallon Builder's original letterhead was rather simple. Rickabaugh Graphics updated Fallon's letterhead to include a logo which varied with different tools.

RALPH W. FALLON
BUILDER, INC.
533 SCHROCK ROAD
COLUMBUS, OHIO 43229
TEL (614) 436-5005
FAX (614) 436-3485

RALPH W. FALLON
BUILDER, INC.
533 SCHROCK ROAD
COLUMBUS, OHIO 43229

Individually Designed and Crafted Homes

Individually Designed and Crafted Homes

Client: **Ralph Fallon Builder, Inc.**
Design Firm: **Rickabaugh Graphics**
                      Gahanna, Ohio

RALPH FALLON BUILDER, INC.

Individually Crafted Homes Since 1926

RALPH FALLON BUILDER, INC.

Individually Crafted Homes Since 1926

533 Schrock Road
Columbus, Ohio 43229

533 Schrock Road   Columbus, Ohio 43229   Telephone 614.436.5005   FAX 614.436.3485

ADVANCED
NETWORK
TECHNOLOGIES

Advanced Network Technologies' old logo looked neither advanced nor very technological. The new logo is more professional in every aspect using a solidly corporate, but creative color scheme.

Client:	**Advanced Network Technologies, Inc.**
Design Firm:	**Cathey Associates, Inc.**
	Dallas, Texas

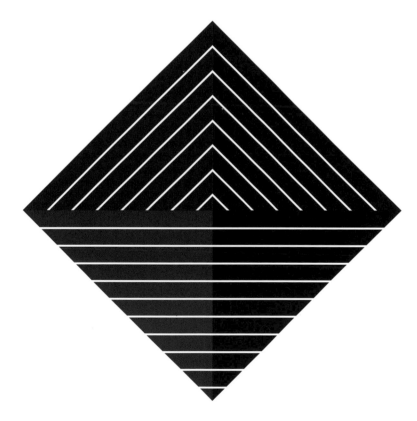

Advanced Network Technologies, Inc.

American Security Mortgage used a clip-art type eagle in its old materials. The new, more distinctive mark combines the star, which helps to say "American", with the form of a contemporary eagle hovering in a protective stance over a home, appropriate for a residential mortgage insurer.

Client: **American Service Mortgage**
Design Firm: **Identity Center**
                Schaumburg, Illinois

The client, Social
Recovery Systems, Inc.,
oversees a number of
outreach and drug
recovery programs, and
asked the designer to
come up with a uniform

A Division of Social Model Recovery Systems, Inc.

PO Box 849
Orange, CA 92666
tel 714 639-5542
fax 714 639-5037

a division of Social Model Recovery Systems, Inc.

Client:
**Social Model
Recovery Systems,
Inc.**
Design Firm:
**Adele Bass &
Company Design**

The River Community   23701 East Fork Road   Azusa   California 91702   (818) 910-1202

identity for all of the programs. To the left are the original identity systems. The revised systems are on this and the following two pages.

SOCIAL MODEL RECOVERY SYSTEMS, INC.

23701 East Fork Road
Azusa, California 91702

(818) 910-1202

fax (818) 910-1380

RIVER COMMUNITY

23701 East Fork Road
Azusa, California 91702
(818) 910-1202
fax (818) 910-1380

Adult Dual Diagnosis
Recovery Services

TOUCHSTONES

P.O. Box 849
Orange, California 92666
(714) 639-5542
fax (714) 639-5037

Adolescent
Alcohol and Other Drug
Recovery Services

ReDesign

Texas Bilingual Association's original two-color letterhead was dated and somewhat unbalanced. The new design represents Texas as well as the U.S., with the book representing education and the star in the letter "A" representing Texas, the lone star state. The colors red, white, and blue represent both Texas and the United States.

PRESIDENT-ELECT
María G. Arias
Socorro ISD
12300 Eastlake Dr.
El Paso, Texas 79927-5400
(915) 860-3458 (wk)
e-mail: marias@socorro.k12.tx.us

PRESIDENT
Dr. Josefina Villamil Tinajero
The Univ. of Texas at El Paso
College of Education
500 W. University Ave.
El Paso, Texas 79968
(915) 747-5552 (wk)
e-mail: tinajero@utep.edu

texas association for bilingual education
* Affiliate of the National Association for Bilingual Education *

Office: 6323 Sovereign Dr. #178 • San Antonio, Texas 78229 • (210) 979-6390 • FAX (210) 979-6485 • 1-800-TABE 930 • TXTABE@aol.com

EXECUTIVE BOARD
1996-1997

Past President
Dr. José A. Ruiz-Escalante
Univ. of Texas at Permian Basin

Vice President
Lupita Hinojosa
Houston I.S.D.

Secretary
Manuel Ruiz III
Edgewood I.S.D.

Treasurer
Eva Ramirez
Univ. of Texas-Pan Am.

Parliamentarian
Raúl O. Ramón
Corpus Christi I.S.D.

Constitution
María J. Chavez
Ector County I.S.D.

Instructional and
Professional Development
R.C. Rodriguez
North East I.S.D.

Legislative
José Angel Hernandez
Houston I.S.D.

Publications and Archives
Dr. Guadalupe Ochoa Thompson
Texas A&M University - Kingsville

Grace Gonzales
Galena Park I.S.D.

Public Relations
Pauline Dow
Canutillo I.S.D.

Elizabeth Varela Lozano
Univ. of Texas at El Paso

Student Representative
Hugo Hernandez
Univ. of Texas at San Antonio

Parent Representative
Lourdes Heredia
Ysleta I.S.D.

Client: **Texas Bilingual Education**
Design Firm: **Juarez Design & Illustration**
                 El Paso, Texas

PRESIDENT
Dr. Josefina Villamil Tinajero
The University of Texas at El Paso
College of Education
500 W. University Ave.
El Paso, Texas 79968
(915) 747-5552 (wk)
E-Mail: tinajero@utep.edu

TEXAS ASSOCIATION FOR BILINGUAL EDUCATION
- Affiliate of the National Association for Bilingual Education

PRESIDENT-ELECT
Maria G. Arias
Socorro I.S.D.
12300 Eastlake Dr.
El Paso, Texas 79927-5400
(915) 860-3458 (wk)
email: marias@socorro.k12.tx.us

Office: 6323 Sovereign Dr. No.178 • San Antonio, Texas 78229 • (210) 979-6390 • FAX (210) 979-6485 • 1-800-TABE-930 • TXTABE@aol.com

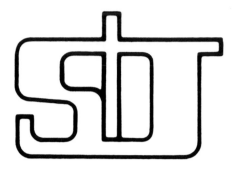

The old identity reflected a somewhat dated, squarish set of letterforms. The goal was to retain a sense of the old, but to add a softness and humanity to the identity. By incorporating a visual of St. Joseph holding the child, in a protective wrapping formed by the "S" and "J", the mark went far beyond the old to depict a gentle, caring atmosphere.

Client: **St. Joseph Hospital—Elgin, Illinois**
Design Firm: **Identity Center**
                    Schaumburg, Illinois

La Leche League International promotes the benefits of natural breastfeeding. The old mark had several deficiencies: it used a very common globe device, lines that were too thin to reproduce well in small sizes, a very thin neck on the woman, and a woman that was not universal enough for an organization that has worldwide representation. The refinement turned the globe into an oval suggestive of an egg, fattened the strokes and softened the woman and child, getting rid of the stiletto fingers.

Client:	**La Leche League International**
Design Firm:	**Identity Center**
	Schaumburg, Illinois

*Re*Design

Flynn Signs and Graphics' old logo was very bold and heavy. The new design was slightly changed with a lighter and more streamlined feel.

EVERYTHING IN SIGNS & LETTERS

3315 E. Anaheim St.
Long Beach, CA 90804
(310) 498-6655   (800) 458-2784
FAX # (310) 985-0843

Client:	**Flynn Signs and Graphics**
Design Firm:	**Damion Hickman Design**
	Newport Beach, California

*Re*Design

Flynn
SINCE 1937
SIGNS & GRAPHICS, INC.

Everything in Signs & Letters
3315 East Anaheim St., Long Beach, CA 90804
(800) 458-2784   (562) 498-6655   **Fax (562) 985-0843**

ReDesign

Castle or Cottage Interiors' old system lacked design quality and the card, letterhead, and envelope bore little or no relation to one another. The new identity system uses a logo across all three pieces to create a single identity.

Castle or Cottage
I n t e r i o r s

5016 South 110 Street

Omaha NE 68137

(402) 592-6905

CASTLE OR COTTAGE INTERIORS
5016 South 110th Street
Omaha, Nebraska 68137-2373

Client: **Castle or Cottage Interiors**
Design Firm: **New Idea Design**
               Omaha, Nebraska

5016 South 110 Street
Omaha, NE 68137
402·592·6905

Jamba Juice needed a fresher and more original identity system. Bright, but organic, colors were chosen along with a freer typeface, logo, and accompanying graphics.

Two of the new designs are shown on the facing page. The others are on the following four pages.

Client: **Jamba Juice**
Design Firm: **Hornall Anderson Design Works**
                        Seattle, Washington

Vantage Communications' existing mark was felt to be too aggressive. By encapsulating the original mark partially—not fully—within a containing shape, more visual mass was added. This reduced the aggressiveness without eliminating the basic dynamic aspects of the original. An affiliate, Image Business Systems, uses the same identifier in a different color scheme. Both company names use a new custom letter styling.

Client: **Vantage Communications**
Design Firm: **Identity Center**
                      Schaumburg, Illinois

Formerly known as McCormick Inn, the hotel was undergoing a coordinated design upgrade timed with a name and identity change to rid itself of the "inn" connotation of inexpensive lodging. The visual identity had to justify the increase in costs reflected by major architectural upgrade.

Client: **McCormick Center Hotel**
Design Firm: **Identity Center**
                 Schaumburg, Illinois

ReDesign

Patricia Sabena's old letterhead lacked design quality and identifying information. The redesign added a logo and essential information such as address and phone. The addition of just one color makes the overall design more emphatic.

Patricia Sabena qualitative research services

Client: **Patricia Sabena**
                 Qualitative Research Services
Design Firm: **Lincoln Design**
                 Eugene, Oregon

Patricia Sabena
Qualitative Research Services

SINCE 1965

Phone: (203) 454-1225
Fax: (203) 221-0180

12 Pequot Trail
Westport, CT 06880

ReDesign

Dr. Carol's old logo did not visually represent her practice. The new logo and letterhead add color and description to her work.

Carol
Joan
McCutcheon
D.D.S.

General Dentistry

621 E. Campbell Ave. #18
Campbell, CA 95008
408/379-0851

Client: Dr. Carol
Design Firm: AERIAL
San Francisco, California

GENERAL, COSMETIC & FAMILY DENTISTRY

Dr. Carol

CAROL McCUTCHEON, DDS, INC. 621 E. CAMPBELL AVE. SUITE 12 CAMPBELL, CA 95008 408/379-0851

CONCORD
Mortgage Corporation, Inc.

Michael Gregg
Loan Manager

1730 Minor Avenue, #103
Seattle, WA 98101

Tel. (206) 467-8000
Fax. (206) 467-6932

Concord Mortgage Company's old logo lacked any design qualities. The new design adds descriptive logo, color, and design to create a package that speaks well for the company.

Client: **Concord Mortgage Corporation**
Design Firm: **Walsh & Associates**
                      Seattle, Washington

Pat Winterton
Senior Loan Consultant

1730 Minor Avenue
Suite 103
Seattle, WA 98101
Tel: 206/467-8000
Fax: 206/467-6932
Pager: 206/340-7901

1730 Minor Avenue

Suite 103

Seattle, WA 98101

Phone:

206/467-8000

Fax:

206/467-6932

Attitude Online had tried to create a logo themselves and asked if Shields could "clean up" the logo. Several versions were created with the "hands-on-hips" look. Then Shields created the figure with arcing electricity, which captures the essence of an Internet provider.

Client: **Attitude Online**
Design Firm: **Shields Design**
                 Fresno, California

ZyLAB produces the leading pc-based text retrieval software and used an identifier combined with a distinctive marketing name. Identity Center created an italic version of the name with a simplified "Z" to suggest the speed of retrieval possible with the product. The new symbol also lent itself to better use as a computer screen icon. The design firm tied the corporate name "ZyLAB" into a coordinated look with the product name "ZyINDEX".

Client:	**ZyLAB**
Design Firm:	**Identity Center**
	Schaumburg, Illinois

ReDesign

HealthPark Dentistry's old logo was beginning to show its age when the owner and 1-earth GRAPHICS worked together to refine the identity system. The tagline was added to further convey the message, while the colors silver and black were used to enhance branding with a color combination associated with a dental practice.

Dentistry - Suite A
110 S. Tippecanoe Drive
Tipp City, OH 45371
(513) 667-2417

...Your Quality Health Connection

Dentistry - Suite A
110 S. Tippecanoe Drive
Tipp City, Ohio 45371

...Your Quality Health Connection

HealthPark is a member of the Samaritan Health Resources network

Client:	**HealthPark Dentistry**
Design Firm:	**1-earth GRAPHICS**
	Troy, Ohio

HealthPARK Dentistry

110 S. Tippecanoe Drive • Suite A
Tipp City, Ohio 45371

(513) 667-2417 • FAX 667-2418

HealthPARK Dentistry

110 S. Tippecanoe Drive

Suite A

Tipp City, Ohio 45371

(513) 667-2417

Caring. Comfortable. Comprehensive. Convenient.

Caring. Comfortable. Comprehensive. Convenient.

The Dayton Flyers' old identity system reflected outdated colors and mismatched designs. The new system integrates colors and logotype to create a coordinated system.

Client: **University of Dayton Flyers**
Design Firm: **Rickabaugh Graphics**
                     Gahanna, Ohio

Re Design

In designing the new letterhead for Goodwin Tucker, a commercial refrigeration and kitchen equipment parts supplier, the designer considered the various elements of the industry. The result was an icon that incorporates actual parts used in repair plus the company's monogram.

GOODWIN TUCKER GROUP

3509 Delaware – P.O. Box 3285 – Des Moines, IA 50316-3285 – (515) 262-9308 – (800) 372-6066

GOODWIN TUCKER GROUP

P. O. BOX 3285
3509 DELAWARE AVE.
DES MOINES, IOWA 50316-3285

CFESA

DES MOINES – WATERLOO – OMAHA – LINCOLN

Client: Goodwin Tucker Group
Design Firm: Sayles Graphic Design
                 Des Moines, Iowa

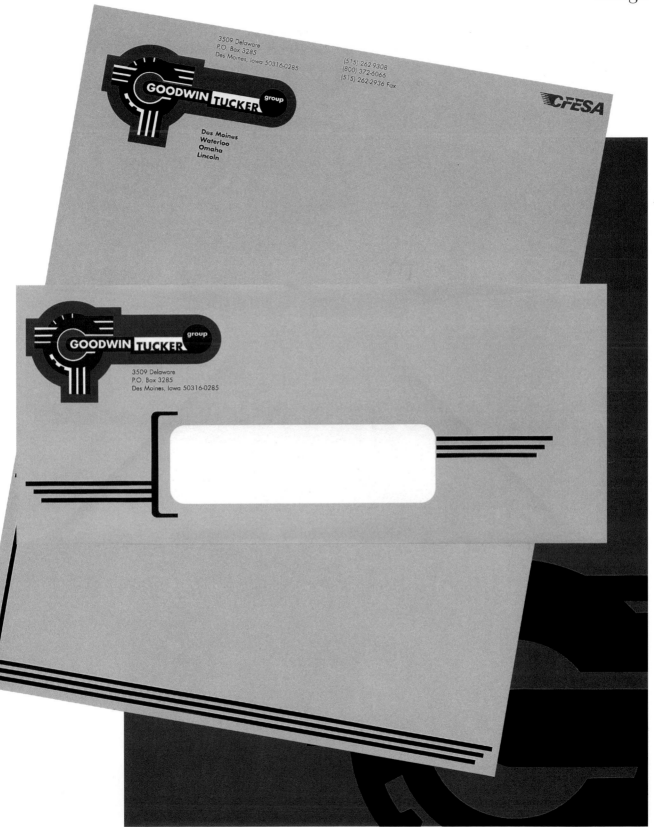

Second Opinion is a one-woman interior design business with a very soft and feminine look. Oddly, the designer's work is bold and contemporary, not soft and delicate, taking chances with unconventional personal statements for her clients. The design is a direct response to her designs.

Client: **Second Opinion Interiors**
Design Firm: **Cathey Associates, Inc.**
                 Dallas, Texas

Radcom, Inc.

Radcom is a telecommunications systems provider who wanted an upgraded identity as it upgraded its services to include telephony, telecomputing, video conferencing, and other new technologies. The old crest is one developed many years ago by the founder's grandfather, who was actually a "snake oil" salesman. (At the top center of the crest is a figure jumping rope and kicking away other health aids. There are even mystic symbols included.) Successfully doing away with the crest was almost painful. The first few ads incorporating the new corporate identity had to include at least a small version of the old crest.

Client: **Radcom**
Design Firm: **Cathey Associates, Inc.**
                 Dallas, Texas

Cutler Travel Marketing's old design used dated colors and looked bland.
In the new design, the globe became the focal point with bold icons of
planes, ships, and destinations interacting with the company's initials.

CTM LC

Incentive and Corporate Group Travel

CTM LC

Incentive and Corporate Group Travel

West Towers • 1200 35th Street • Suite 208
West Des Moines, Iowa 50266

CUTLER TRAVEL MARKETING
We *Work* For You!

West Towers • 1200 35th Street • Suite 208 • West Des Moines, Iowa 50266
(515) 226-9348 / fax (515) 226-9112

Client: **Cutler Travel Marketing**
Design Firm: **Sayles Graphic Design**
              Des Moines, Iowa

CUTLER TRAVEL MARKETING

Incentive and Corporate Group Travel

1200 35th Street, Suite 208   West Des Moines, Iowa 50266   515-226-9348   fax-226-9112

CTM

ReDesign

After Hours Creative's old letterhead was very expressive, yet
included no essential information such as name, phone, or address.
The new design keeps the "late night" theme, and includes the needed
information.

Client: **After Hours Creative**
Design Firm: **After Hours Creative**
                  Phoenix, Arizona

AFTER | HOURS
CREATIVE

PHOENIX ARIZONA 85034
1201 E JEFFERSON 100B
CREATIVE
AFTER|

602
P 2 5 6 2 6 4 8 | F 2 5 6 6 4 2 2

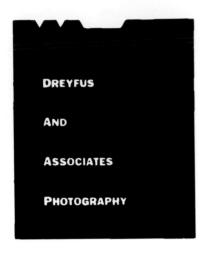

dreyfus & associates' old logo was plain and lacked personality. The redesign creates a lively image for this photography studio.

Client: **dreyfus & associates photography**
Design Firm: **CUBE Advertising/Design**
                 St. Louis, Missouri

PRODUCTIVE ASSISTANCE

This small programming and software publishing company specializes in assisting businesses implement the new technologies of computer automation and data management. Cathey Associates replaced the Copperplate signature with a corporate name commensurate with Data Launch's services and the current state of the art.

Client: **Data Launch**
Design Firm: **Cathey Associates, Inc.**
                 Dallas, Texas

DATA LAUNCH

ReDesign

Deleo Clay Tile's letterhead was colorful and represented the business well, but lacked character. The new design has a warmth and solidness absent in the original.

DELEO·CLAY·TILE

600
CHANEY
STREET
—
LAKE ELSINORE,
CALIFORNIA
92330
—
(714) 674-1578

Client: **Deleo Clay Tile**
Design Firm: **Mires Design**
               San Diego, California

Re Design

Alpine Press's old letterhead seemed antiquated and primitive. The redesign kept the pine tree, but incorporated the monogram into the mountain and tree. The result is much more professional and representative of a press.

Client: **Alpine Press**
Design Firm: **Lincoln Design**
               Eugene, Oregon

ALPINE PRESS
INCORPORATED

91 North Main Street (rear)   Norwalk, Connecticut 06854   (203) 853-0043   Fax (203) 855-9966

Burley Design Cooperative's old logo was a bit staid and lacked punch. The new logo kept the eye-catching yellow, but used a graphic accurately representing a cooperative.

Client: **Burley Design Cooperative**
Design Firm: **Funk & Associates**
Eugene, Oregon

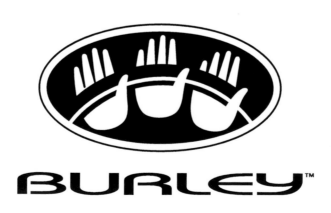

74

Eugene Area Chamber of Commerce's old logo used a dated typeface and lines that would not reproduce well at small sizes. Keeping the essence of the old graphic, the new design is bolder and is paired with a timeless typeface.

Client: Eugene Area Chamber of Commerce
Design Firm: Funk & Associates
                 Eugene, Oregon

Eugene Area Chamber of Commerce

Eugene Area Chamber of Commerce

Rhino Chasers' new logo was rendered in an illustrative, almost woodcut style. Distinct packaging colors identify different products.

Client: **Rhino Chasers**
Design Firm: **Hornall Anderson Design Works**
                       Seattle, Washington

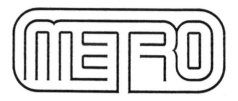

Thirteen years before the latter, this design firm did the first logo version when Metro Transportation Group was founded. The transportation planning company experienced considerable growth and gave Identity Center the opportunity to refine the mark, adding more visual mass and refining the lower left portion into a more distinctive form.

Client: **Metro Transportation Group**
Design Firm: **Identity Center**
Schaumburg, Illinois

Atticus Scribe's old logo was complex. The redesign better reflects the business with the column merging into a pencil point.

Client: **Atticus Scribe**
Design Firm: **Rickabaugh Graphics**
                 Gahanna, Ohio

ReDesign

HealthGate's original design lacked design quality and was very dated. The colors of the design were trendy in the 1970s, but the letterhead needed to be brought into the 21st century. The redesign added a logo while updating the typeface and design.

HealthGate™ Data Corp.
380 PLEASANT STREET, SUITE 230
MALDEN, MA 02148
http://www.healthgate.com • info@healthgate.com

800-434-GATE
617-321-2262 FAX

Client: **HealthGate Data Corp.**
Design Firm: **Stewart Monderer Design**
                        Boston, Massachusetts

HealthGate™ DATA CORP.

380 Pleasant Street, Suite 230
Malden, Massachusetts 02148-8123
Tel: 617 321 6000
Fax: 617 321 2262
Web: http://www.healthgate.com

ReDesign

Print Media & Design's old stationery system was only one year old when the client, tired of the design, sought a new system. The client wanted a logo and stationery system that reflected her personality, yet represented her studio as solid and established.

PRINT MEDIA & DESIGN, INC.

701 E Street, SE
Suite 100
Washington, DC 20003
Ph: 202.544.8601
Fx: 202.544.8603

Client: **Print Media & Design**
Design Firm: **Steve Trapero Design**
Silver Spring, Maryland

PRINT MEDIA & DESIGN, INC.

701 E. STREET, SE, SUITE 100
WASHINGTON, DC 20003
· 2 0 2 · 5 4 4 · 8 6 0 1
FAX 202·544·8603
E-MAIL pmdezin@mail.idt.net

Willamette Valley Company's old logo was hard to read and looked
outdated. The new version is also an "initial" logo, but simplifies it to a
memorable "W."

Client: **Willamette Valley Company**
Design Firm: **Funk & Associates**
                 Eugene, Oregon

W V C O

W V C O

Orenco Systems' old logo was easy to read, but did not reflect the company's business. The new version uses clean lines, waves, and dots in order to convey the company's filter business.

Client: **Orenco Systems**
Design Firm: **Funk & Associates**
                  Eugene, Oregon

Orenco Systems®
Incorporated

Northwest Vending Company's old letterhead badly needed updating.
The new version is more open and much cleaner.

Client: **PepsiCola Bottling Company of Eugene**
Design Firm: **Lincoln Design**
           Eugene, Oregon

732 Shelley Street • Springfield, OR 97477

732 Shelley Street • Springfield, Oregon 97477
(541) 726-0991 • FAX (541) 746-6423 • (800) 452-9585

Re Design

Seattle Goodwill's old design was lackluster and outdated. The redesign added a new, expressive logo and color to make the identity system exciting.

Seattle Goodwill Industries • 1400 South Lane Street • Seattle, Washington 98144-2889 • (206) 329-1000

Client: Seattle Goodwill
Design Firm: Hansen Design Company, Inc.
                 Seattle, Washington

Seattle
Goodwill

GILBERT RECYCLED
25% COTTON

Education at Work
1400 South Lane Street ~ Seattle, WA 98144.2889
Tel. 206.329.1000 ~ Fax 206.726.1502

RU Computing was a small but successful network integration firm that decided to invest in rapid growth. Though the name was cute, it was simply inadequate to account for any growth. The new version includes a total name change and new methodology for presenting corporate identity.

Client: **Axxys Technologies**
Design Firm: **Cathey Associates, Inc.**
                  Dallas, Texas

A name change necessitated a logo change for the Oregon University System. The new logo has a feel that looks to the future as the orbiting "O" creates movement within the logo.

Client: **Oregon University System**
Design Firm: **Funk & Associates**
                      Eugene, Oregon

Oregon
University
System

Oregon
University
System

Design

GeoCapital's logo lacked emphasis. The new design added focus by using geometric shapes and color.

GEOCAPITAL™

FAX (212) 486-4469

GeoCapital Corporation, 767 Fifth Avenue, New York, New York 10153/(212) 486-4455

Client:	GeoCapital
Design Firm:	Quon/Designation Inc.
	New York, New York

Pepsi's old packaging had been in use for some time and needed some updating. The new package used the same colors and kept the Pepsi logo, but highlighted the word "diet" more than past packaging had done.

Client: Pepsi Cola Company
Design Firm: Hornall Anderson Design Works
                 Seattle, Washington

ReDesign

Goodtime Jazz Festival's old letterhead reflected the festival, but lacked personality. The redesign kept the same colors and the musicians, but chose multiple typefaces to compliment the New Orleans flavor of the festival.

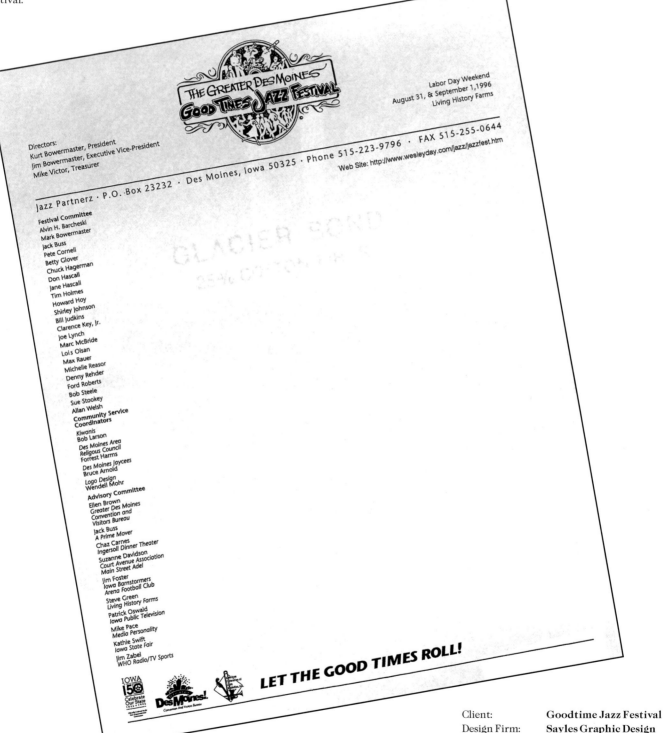

Client: **Goodtime Jazz Festival**
Design Firm: **Sayles Graphic Design**
Des Moines, Iowa

THE GREATER ★ DES MOINES
GOOD ★ TIMES
Jazz Festival ★
DOWNTOWN DES MOINES
LABOR DAY WEEKEND
AUGUST 29, 30 & 31 1997
MAIN VENUE: CONVENTION CENTER

DIRECTORS
KURT BOWERMASTER President
JIM BOWERMASTER Executive Vice President
MIKE VICTOR Treasurer

JAZZ PARTNERZ
P.O. Box 23232
Des Moines, Iowa 50325
Phone (515) 223-9796
Fax (515) 255-0844
Web Site
www.wesleyday.com/jazzfest

FESTIVAL COMMITTEE
Bruce Arnold
Vel Bablchuk
Alvin H. Barcheski
Mark Bowermaster
Jack Buss
Jon Dickerson
Phyllis Eggspuehler
Chuck Hagerman
Don Hascall
Jane Hascall
Tim Holmes
Howard Hoy
Betty Hufford
Shirley Johnson
Bill Judkins
Jack Kiburz
Joe Lynch
Jane Mahaffey
Larry Mahaffey
Lois Olson
Gene Raffensperger
Max Rauer
Michelle Reasor
Denny Rehder
Jenny Rehder
Ford Roberts
John Smith
Bob Steele
Jerry Van Zee
Betty Van Zee
Bob Wanarka

JAZZ RUN
Jim Fliehler

SECOND LINE
JO BERRY

GRAPHICS
SAYLES GRAPHIC DESIGN

ADVISORY COMMITTEE
ELLEN BROWN
Greater Des Moines Convention and Visitors Bureau

CHAZ CARNES
Ingersoll Dinner Theater

SUZANNE DAVIDSON
Court Avenue Association

JIM FOSTER
Iowa Barnstormers Arena Football Club

MIKE PACE
Media Personality

KATHIE SWIFT
Iowa State Fair

JIM ZABEL
WHO Radio / TV Sports

"Let the GOOD ★ TIMES roll"

GREATER DES MOINES CONVENTION AND VISITORS BUREAU

DOWNTOWN PARTNERSHIP, INC.

Clayco Construction's old logo was a bit confusing. The new design, which included only minor changes, made the Clayco name more readable.

Client: **Clayco Construction**
Design Firm: **CUBE Advertising/Design**
                  St. Louis, Missouri

This Florida company produces a series of ostomy-related products. Since the family imagery was used in the old mark, Identity Center's goal was to develop a new version which retained a hint of the old. The new mark combines the letter "U" with a family formed by several positive and negative strokes. The heads of the children also highlight the abdominal area of the man and woman, which is the focus of the company's products.

Client: **United Medical**
Design Firm: **Identity Center**
                 Schaumburg, Illinois

Design

Servoss Public Relations & Marketing's old letterhead was plain and
dated. Although a name change necessitated the letterhead change, the
redesign adds color and punch to the Servoss image.

SERVOSS
PUBLIC RELATIONS & MARKETING

455 SHERMAN ST., SUITE 455, DENVER, CO 80203   303•777•6200 FAX: 303•744•7541
PARTNER, PINNACLE WORLDWIDE, INC.
Offices in Atlanta, Boston, Chicago, Cleveland, Costa Mesa, Dallas, Detroit, Houston, Kansas City, Los Angeles, Miami, Minneapolis, New York, Philadelphia, Portland, San Francisco, St. Louis,
Tampa, Toronto, Washington, Barcelona, Bern, Bilbao, Breda, Brussels, Copenhagen, Dublin, Frankfurt, The Hague, Helsinki, Lisbon, Madrid, Manchester, Moscow,
Paris/Versailles, Rome, Sevilla, Valencia, Vienna, Auckland, Singapore, Sydney, Tokyo, Cairo, Tel Aviv, Mexico City, and Sao Paulo

Client: **Servoss Public Relations**
Design Firm: **Ellen Bruss Design**
                     Denver, Colorado

SERVOSS | CHARNEY

PUBLIC RELATIONS & MARKETING

*Re*Design

Des Moines Plumbing's old letterhead was outdated and had no
personality. The new design is exciting and colorful.

DES MOINES PLUMBING

515-243-5111

1501 Michigan Ave. • Des Moines, Iowa 50314

Fax 515-243-1784

REMODELING • NEW CONSTRUCTION
BACKHOE

*"Providing Quality,
Reliability, and
Performance."*

Client: **Des Moines Plumbing**
Design Firm: **Sayles Graphic Design**
                 Des Moines, Iowa

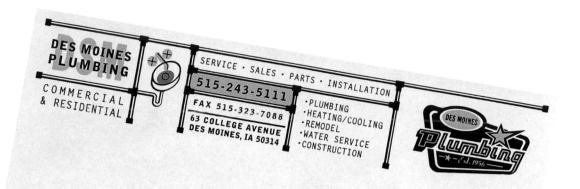

DES MOINES PLUMBING

DSM

COMMERCIAL
& RESIDENTIAL

SERVICE · SALES · PARTS · INSTALLATION

515-243-5111

FAX 515-323-7088

63 COLLEGE AVENUE
DES MOINES, IA 50314

· PLUMBING
· HEATING/COOLING
· REMODEL
· WATER SERVICE
· CONSTRUCTION

DES MOINES
Plumbing
Est. 1956

Gotcha's old logo was effective, but the surf clothing company needed a logo to keep up with their cutting edge image.

Client: **Gotcha Sportswear**
Design Firm: **Mike Salisbury Communications**
                   Torrance, California

ThermoCouple Products needed a much stronger, more distinctive "TCP" than the old mark. The three colors introduced as squares within the mark are also used distinctively in applications to suggest the three service areas of the company.

Client: **ThermoCouple Products**
Design Firm: **Identity Center**
               Schaumburg, Illinois

Design

Tri-County Board of Recovery and Mental Health Services old system was plain and needed a logo. 1-earth GRAPHICS designed a logo and stationery system that emphasizes the Board's main mission: mental health care for people in three counties.

Tri-County Board of Recovery & Mental Health Services

405 Public Square • Suite 330 • Troy, Ohio 45373 • Phone (513) 335-7727 • FAX (513) 335-8816

Serving the people of Darke, Miami and Shelby Counties
An equal opportunity employer

Client: Tri-County Board of Recovery
                & Mental Health Services
Design Firm: 1-earth GRAPHICS
                Troy, Ohio

Tri-County Board
of Recovery & Mental Health Services

405 Public Square • Suite 330 • Troy, OH 45373 • (937) 335-7727 • 1-800-589-2853 • FAX (937) 335-8816

• Serving the people of Darke, Miami & Shelby Counties • An Equal Opportunity Employer •

*Re*Design

Laguna Beach Art Museum's old logo had no relationship to the location or the art in the museum. The new logo uses the color of the natural environment and a logo that reflects the impressionist style of the collection.

Client: **Laguna Beach Art Museum**
Design Firm: **Mike Salisbury Communications**
Torrance, California

LAGUNA ART MUSEUM

307 CLIFF DRIVE LAGUNA BEACH, CA 92651-9990 (714) 494-8971 FAX (714) 494-1530

Hot Rod Hell's old logo was cost effective, but not visually effective. The new design keeps the basic image, but offers a not-quite-as-wicked-looking devil. Added color and effectively-used type create a more professional image for the store.

Client: **Hot Rod Hell**
Design Firm: **Mires Design**
                    San Diego, California

*Re*Design

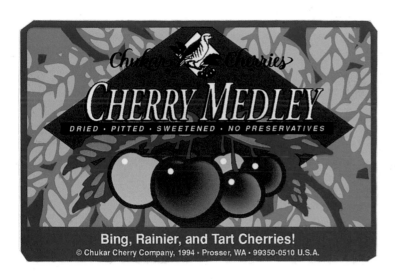

Chukar Cherries' old logo was sterile, lacked personality, and was not memorable. The new logo brings personality and energy to the company, while giving the line continuity.

Client: **Chukar Cherries**
Design Firm: **Walsh & Associates**
               Seattle, Washington

Bodycology

Bodycology's old logo used a script typeface that was difficult to read. The redesign uses a more readable script and emphasizes it by reversing it out of a dark background.

Client: **Bodycology**
Design Firm: **Shimokochi/Reeves**
                 Los Angeles, California

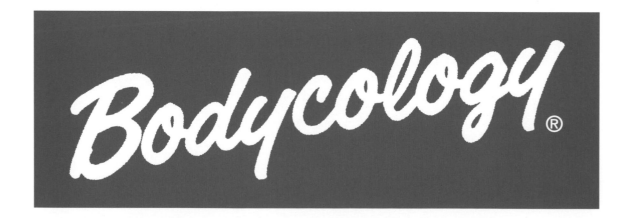

All Tool markets brake lathes that appear with the identity in brake shops. The old mark had the makings of a good identifier, but needed a slight change to make it more distinctive. Equally important to the "make-over" were refinements to the way the name was shown. The square "O"s created a stodgy look, so they were refined and combined with a "T" form that was repeated within the symbol itself. The triangular "feet" were added to the "A" to give a more solid mass to the symbol.

Client:	**All Tool**
Design Firm:	**Identity Center**
	Schaumburg, Illinois

ReDesign

The Printing Stations' old letterhead looked dated and did not represent the store's capabilities. The redesign used elements familiar to printers: registration marks and the image of cylinders of a printing press to create a lively letterhead the represents the business.

1023 GRAND AVENUE · DES MOINES, IOWA 50309 · (515) 243-8144

QUICK PRINTING · COPYING · TYPESETTING · BINDERY SERVICES · AND MORE!

Client: **Printing Station**
Design Firm: **Sayles Graphic Design**
Des Moines, Iowa

PRINTING
STATION
P·S

1420 LOCUST
DES MOINES, IOWA 50309
515-243-8144
FAX 243-6540

*Re*Design

Adventure Lighting's old letterhead system was staid, and did not accurately represent the company's image. The new system kept the lighthouse, but used a more colorful, exciting design to convey the company's identity.

Adventure Lighting

750 E. Elm Street ○ Des Moines, Iowa 50309 ○ 515-288-0444

Client:	**Adventure Lighting**
Design Firm:	**Sayles Graphic Design**
	Des Moines, Iowa

ADVENTURE LIGHTING

90 Washington Avenue
Des Moines, Iowa 50314
515-288-0444 • Fax 288-1934

PC FIXX, INC.™

PC Fixx's old logo was plain and had no brand equity. The new logo needed to upgrade the image to show that their facilities and products had been upgraded.

Client: **PC Fixx**
Design Firm: **Walsh & Associates**
                 Seattle, Washington

ReDesign

SpringMeade felt that the graphic window on white stock was too cold and did not convey the spirit of the retirement community. The new logo includes a rendering of the tree-lined lane as you enter the community and uses cream stock to create warmth.

4385 South County Road 25A
Tipp City, Ohio 45371
(513) 667-1811

Client: **SpringMeade Retirement Community**
Design Firm: **1-earth GRAPHICS**
Troy, Ohio

Design

Cross America's traditional letterhead did not convey the "Old world sense. New world ideas." image the company has. The new letterhead incorporates the monogram "C" with a globe graphic and complementing typestyle. A riblaid paper imparts a subtly conservative look.

6979 UNIVERSITY AVENUE
DES MOINES, IOWA 50311-1540
515-255-7352   800-728-3829   FAX 515-255-7983

Client: Cross America
Design Firm: Sayles Graphic Design
                      Des Moines, Iowa

6979 University Avenue
Des Moines, Iowa 50311

(515) 255-7352
(800) 728-3829

Fax (515) 255-7983

CROSS
AMERICA
CORPORATION

Old
world
sense.
New
world
ideas.

Tokyo Broadcasting System's old logo was colorless and hard to read, giving the station a lifeless image. The new version added color and life to the station's image.

Client: **Tokyo Broadcasting System**
Design Firm: **Shimokochi/Reeves**
                    Los Angeles, California

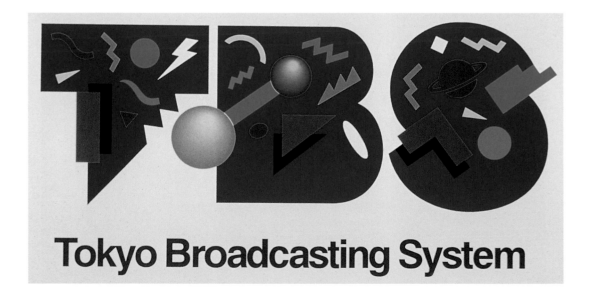

The company's old mark was very busy visually, and used thin strokes which disappeared in small use or when viewed from a distance. The new simplified mark imprints the name "Belden" and at the same time uses three simple dots to strongly imply the bricks for which the company is known.

Client: The Belden Brick Company
Design Firm: Identity Center
                 Schaumburg, Illinois

BEL:DEN

The Village Recorder image was stuck in a time warp. The new design brought them into the 21st century with panache.

Client: **The Village Recorder**
Design Firm: **Mike Salisbury Communications**
Torrance, California

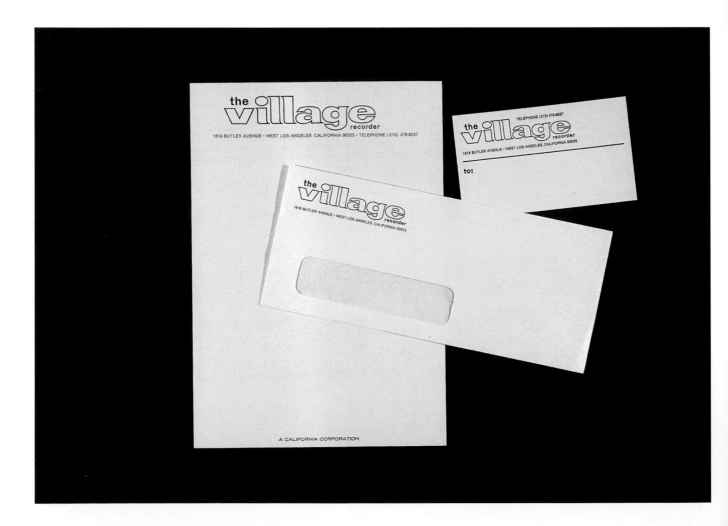

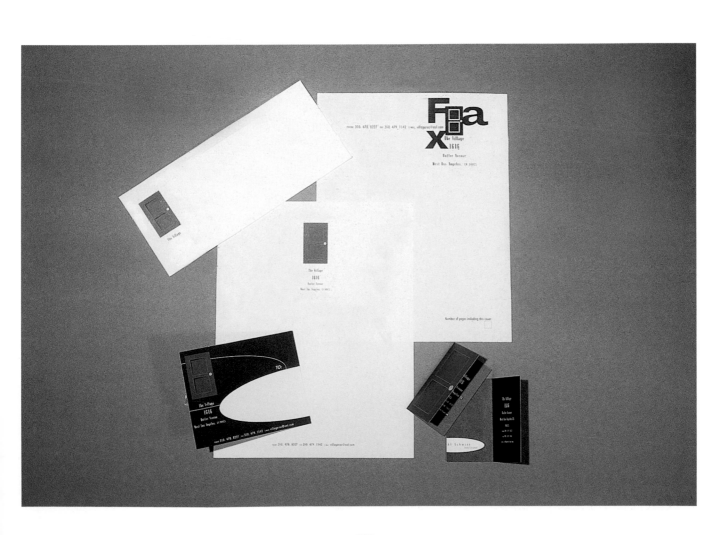

ReDesign

The Iowa Chapter of the American Marketing Association wanted to update their image. The result is a funky logo with bright colors.

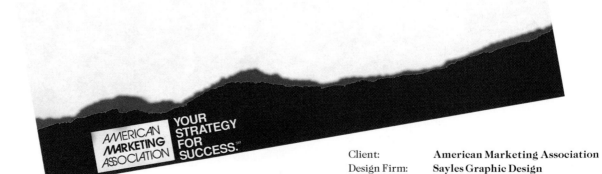

Client:	**American Marketing Association**
Design Firm:	**Sayles Graphic Design**
	Des Moines, Iowa

P.O. BOX

7367

DES MOINES

IOWA

50309

IOWA
CHAPTER

www.ama.org/chapter/c099/

AM ERICAN
MA RKETING
ASS OCIA TION

GREEN GARDEN FOODS

Green Garden Foods' old logo was blocky and hard-edged. The new logo has more of an organic shape with italic type and negative-space swirl that suggest progression and movement.

Client: **Green Garden Foods**
Design Firm: **Walsh & Associates**
                Seattle, Washington

With a name like Roselle, the village used the obvious rose motif. Since the single rose is a common design, with some excellent versions in the marketplace, Identity Center decided to interweave three roses creating a more unusual, yet stronger, visual mass. To complete the logo, two supporting stems in the form of people were added.

Client: **Village of Roselle, Illinois**
Design Firm: **Identity Center**
                    Schaumburg, Illinois

*Re*Design

Adventure 16's old identity was sterile and somewhat outdated. The new design creates a lively identity that reflects the nature of the business.

Client: **Adventure 16**
Design Firm: **Mires Design**
                    San Diego, California

The Natural Way's old logo was static. The redesign used only minor modifications, but created an exciting logo with movement.

Client: **The Natural Way**
Design Firm: **CUBE Advertising/Design**
                 St. Louis, Missouri

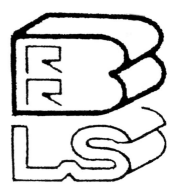

R.R. Brink Locking Systems started with a weak rendition that tried to get all the letters of the name into the act. The design firm's goals were to limit the letters to that of the key name to remember—Brink—and to reflect the primary business of locking systems.

Client: **R.R. Brink Locking Systems, Inc.**
Design Firm: **Identity Center**
               Schaumburg, Illinois

*Re*Design

The Loop Corporation's old letterhead was complex with the relationship
between graphic elements looking forced. The new design went with a
simpler design and softer colors.

Client: **The Loop Corporation**
Design Firm: **Hansen Design Company**
                 Seattle, Washington

The Loop Corporation
568 First Avenue South
Seattle, WA 98104
Telephone: 206.624.2372
Fax: 206.624.2135

Strathmore

PURE COTTON

Re Design

Culinary Arts & Entertainment's old letterhead and logo reflected the Taste of Phoenix well, but a name change necessitated a logo change. The result is a logo that incorporates the initials C, A, and E into a cafe sign.

METROPOLITAN PRESS, INC.

7610 East McDonald Drive, Suite F • Scottsdale, Arizona 85250 • (602) 998-5810 Fax (602) 998-9064

Client: **Culinary Arts & Entertainment**
Design Firm: **After Hours Creative**
Phoenix, Arizona

culinary arts & entertainment

7610 e. mcdonald dr. suite h, scottsdale, az 85250

tel: 602 998 5810 tel: 800 211 5844 fax: 602 998 9064

The Graduate School of Library Information Science's old logo was complex but dated-looking. The new logo uses the seal format and look, but creates a modern-looking logo.

Client: **Graduate School of Library Information Science**
Design Firm: **Shimokochi/Reeves**
                 Los Angeles, California

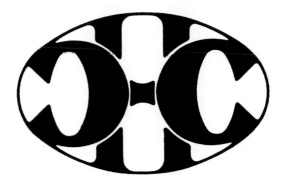

C.H. Compton, Inc., made presentation binders which were often well beyond the ordinary, off-the-shelf binder. Their CHC mark was in itself not a bad looking mark, but the large "H" was inappropriate and had nothing to do with what Compton did. The client accepted a proposed name change, along with the new "C" design, which used multistroke forms to suggest presentation materials that were bound along an edge. To further imprint the name and visually tie it to the mark, the triple white stroke was carried into the name "Compton".

Client: **Compton Presentation Systems**
Design Firm: **Identity Center**
               Schaumburg, Illinois

Design

Executive Strategies' old logo badly needed updating to convey the breakthrough image of the company. The resulting design incorporates the letter "e" and a stylized arrow into a modern design that represents the image.

Susan B. Wilson, M.B.A.
1105 West 12th Street South, Newton, Iowa 50208
Telephone 515-791-7904 ▲ FAX 515-792-1956 ▲ Online SusWilson @ aol.

Client: **Executive Strategies**
Design Firm: **Sayles Graphic Design**
               Des Moines, Iowa

EXECUTIVE STRATEGIES

BREAKTHROUGHS FOR
POWER AND PROFIT

1105 W. 12TH STREET SOUTH
NEWTON, IOWA 50208

515 791 7904
888 246 GOAL
FAX 515 792 1956
ONLINE suwilson@netins.net

Seattle Chocolates' old packaging had few variations: different colors for different flavors. The new packaging uses different styles for different seasons and uses a new logo on the package.

Client: **Seattle Chocolates**
Design Firm: **Hornall Anderson Design Works**
                 Seattle, Washington

Design

Mid America Search's old letterhead and logo were outdated and boring.
The new identity kept the same arrow design, but brought it into the
21st century by reflecting e-mail and fax.

 MID AMERICA SEARCH
Three Fountains Office Park, Suite 226   4401 Westown Parkway
West Des Moines, Iowa 50266-6721   Phone: 515-225-1942   Fax: 515-225-3941

Client: **Mid America Search**
Design Firm: **Sayles Graphic Design**
                     Des Moines, Iowa

MID AMERICA SEARCH

4401 Westown Parkway, Suite 226
West Des Moines, Iowa 50266-6721

(515) 225-1942
Fax (515) 225-3941

Brightwater

E mail mas@dwx.com

UNITED PIPE & SUPPLY CO., INC.

JOHN W. PETERSON, III
REGIONAL MANAGER

CORPORATE OFFICE
90099 PRAIRIE ROAD
P.O. BOX 2220
EUGENE, OREGON 97402
FAX (541) 688-5988
(800) 288-6511
PAGER (541) 341-2757

BRANCHES
THROUGHOUT
THE NORTHWEST

United Pipe and Supply's old logo used an outdated type and design. The new version makes use of a timeless typeface and updates the graphic for the 21st century.

Client: **United Pipe and Supply**
Design Firm: **Funk & Associates**
                       Eugene, Oregon

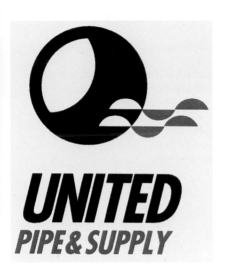

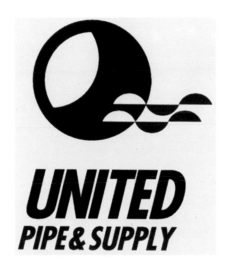

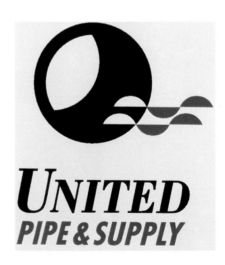

Pacific World's original logo used an awkward piece of art and a dated typeface. The new version's art emphasizes the world in Pacific World and uses a timeless typeface.

Client: **Pacific World**
Design Firm: **Shimokochi/Reeves**
Los Angeles, California

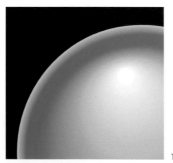

PACIFIC WORLD

ande·mac design

● *fabrics*

● *environmental graphics and*

interiors

(206) 285-6098

Ande Mac Design's old logo used a nice image, but it had no relationship to the name. The new logo incorporates a ribboning graphic into the initial "A".

Client: **Ande Mac Design**
Design Firm: **Walsh & Associates**
                 Seattle, Washington

*Re*Design

Hotel Fort Des Moines' old logo and letterhead used a dated, lackluster design. The new version keeps the image of the hotel as the logo, but adds decorative type and colors to set the ambiance for the hotel.

Hotel Fort Des Moines

Classic Inn

1000 WALNUT STREET • DES MOINES • IOWA 50309 • (515) 243-1161 • TOLL FREE: 1 (800) 532-1466 • FAX (515) 243-4317

Client: **Hotel Fort Des Moines**
Design Firm: **Sayles Graphic Design**
                  Des Moines, Iowa

Hotel Fort Des Moines
1000 Walnut Street
Des Moines, Iowa 50309

Phone: (515) 243-1161
Fax: (515) 243-4317
Reservations: (800) 532-1466

HOTEL·FORT
DeJ MoINeJ

Abby's Legendary Pizza used a variety of identities, though many involved a shield design. The new version kept the shield design, but updated it, reflecting both the brand equity of Abby's and bringing it into the future.

Client: **Abby's Legendary Pizza**
Design Firm: **Funk & Associates**
                        Eugene, Oregon

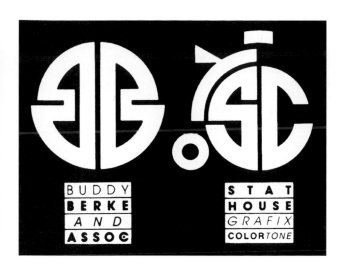

Originally, this traditional stat company employed a confusing collection of various names. All of a sudden the business found itself in the electronic age. Mike Salisbury Communications put all of the aliases in one file, "Power House", for which the logo was created. The new name is easier to remember, at the same time relating to newer, younger clients.

Client: **Powerhouse**
Design Firm: **Mike Salisbury Communications**
                 Torrance, California

Design

Barrack's original letterhead system had no equity and looked thrown together. The new system makes use of a memorable logo and a design carried throughout the system.

Barrick Roofing & Sheet Metal, Inc.
Established 1878

Commercial & Industrial Roofing
Architectural Sheet Metal
Fax (515) 244-3557

10 COLLEGE AVENUE
DES MOINES, IOWA 50314-3519
Ph. (515) 244-3513

Client: **Barrack Roofing & Sheetmetal**
Design Firm: **Sayles Graphic Design**
                    Des Moines, Iowa

10
COLLEGE AVE.

DES MOINES
IOWA 50314

"We're on top of things"

PHONE
(515) 244-3513

FAX
(515) 244-3557

FOUNDED
IN
1878

ReDesign

Fran's Chocolates' old logo and brochure were outdated, used only two colors, and offered drawings of products instead of photography. The new brochure used four-color photography to give an accurate image of the product.

Client: **Fran's Chocolates**
Design Firm: **Walsh & Associates**
               Seattle, Washington

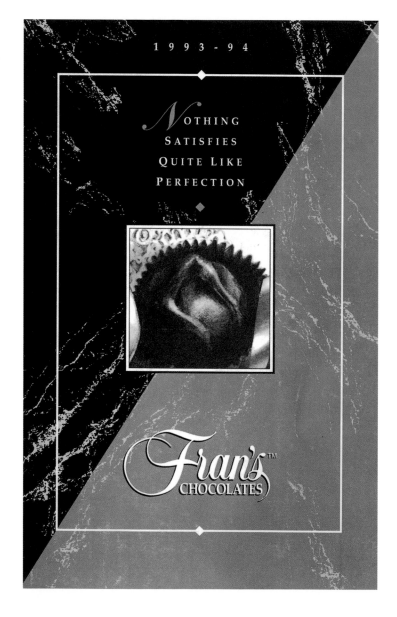

States Industries' old logo used type only and did not stand out in a crowd. The new design makes use of a triangular logotype imposed above the name.

Client: **States Industries**
Design Firm: **Funk & Associates**
                        Eugene, Oregon

VersaLogic CORP.

VersaLogic's old logo looked plain and somewhat outdated. The new logo catches up with the times by using a classic typeface in conjunction with a graphic resembling a circuitboard.

Client: **VersaLogic Corporation**
Design Firm: **Funk & Associates**
                 Eugene, Oregon

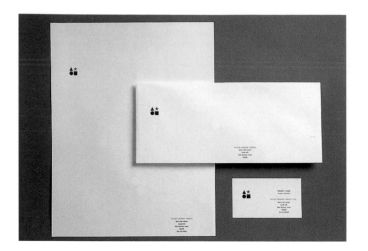

This spread shows the evolution of a design. Sayles Graphic Design's original logo was effective, but looked rather ordinary. Red scribbling with a negative-space star was an improvement in style and memorability. The newest design utilizes additional color and very bold graphics to create even more personality.

Client: **Sayles Graphic Design**
Design Firm: **Sayles Graphic Design**
Des Moines, Iowa

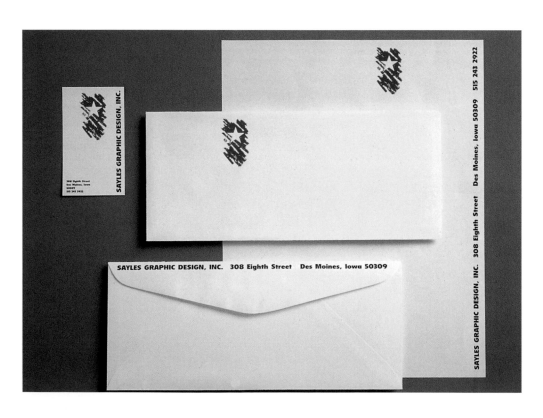

308 Eighth Street Des Moines, Iowa 50309 515-243-2922 Fax 243-0212

Design

Arc Abrasives' letterhead badly needed to be brought into the 90s.
1-earth GRAPHICS refined the old logo by changing the typeface
and adding a subtle drop shadow behind the graphic.

Client: Arc Abrasives, Inc.
Design Firm: 1-earth GRAPHICS
                Troy, Ohio

Delivering the finishing touch.

Delivering the finishing touch.

85 Marybill Drive • Box 10 • Troy, OH 45373

85 Marybill Drive • Box 10 • Troy, OH 45373
PH (513) 335-5607 • 1-800-888-4885 • FAX 1-800-888-4969
INTERNET • http://www.industry.net/arcabrasives

INTEGRATED CONCEPTS, INC.

Integrated Concepts is a large network integration company that was functioning with a "mom and pop" look. The company actually works in the cutting edge of technology and is the partner of other high-tech companies, such as an internet service provider. The aim of the design was to set them apart from the crowd of little integrators and to provide a look within which they can grow into the next century.

Client: **Integrated Concepts Incorporated**
Design Firm: **Cathey Associates, Inc.**
Dallas, Texas

Infinet is a network integration firm that was in need of visual design refinement. Cathey Associates decided to keep the infinity as a conceptual icon, but to simplify the visual messages in the logo. When production techniques allow, the new infinity symbol is shiny gold.

Client: **Infinet Incorporated**
Design Firm: **Cathey Associates, Inc.**
                 Dallas, Texas

ReDesign

Calypso's original letterhead and logo included a splash of color that reflected the business. However, the logo and design were dated. In the new design, AERIAL has created a new, exciting logo that expresses both the name and the business.

CALYPSO COLOR·LABS

CLASSIC CREST

2000 Martin Ave., Santa Clara, CA 95050 (408) 727-2318

Client: Calypso
Design Firm: A E R I A L
                        San Francisco, California

CALYPSO IMAGING, INC.

2000 MARTIN AVENUE

SANTA CLARA, CALIFORNIA

TEL 408.727.2318
TOLL FREE 800.794.2755
FAX 408.727.1705

ZIP 95050.2700

*Re*Design

CNA Architecture's simplistic design lacked character. The redesign incorporates a new logo and colors to create a more interesting and refined appearance.

CNA
Architecture

777 108th NE #400
Bellevue WA 98004-5118
206-822-6700
Fax: 206-828-9116

Arlan E. Collins
Keith A. Null
Mark L. Woerman, AIA
Principal Architects

Client: **CNA Architecture**
Design Firm: **Hansen Design Company, Inc.**
                    Seattle, Washington

ARCHITECTURE

CNA Architecture Inc.
777 108th NE #400
Bellevue WA 98004-5118

Tel 425.822.6700
Fax 425.828.9116

Principal Architects:
Arlan E. Collins
Keith A. Null
Mark L. Woerman, AIA

District 211's old mark used a cross-type device separating traditional elements in a shield motif. However, the words within the mark were too small to be read except in very large applications. Since the 211 used two "1"s, it seemed natural to develop a mark using the numerals, making both the ones students. The simplified 211 works well on the district's fleet of 200 buses and other vehicles.

Client: **Township High School District 211**
Design Firm: **Identity Center**
                      Schaumburg, Illinois

District 214 is the second largest high school district in Illinois, and it used somewhat ordinary numerals for its identifier. Identity Center's solution tried to reflect a hint of the old mark, but to also refine and add meaning to the symbol beyond just the numerals. In this case, the upward stroke of the "4" points to the sun as the "bright future on the horizon" for the student looking toward the future.

Client: **Township High School District 214**
Design Firm: **Identity Center**
                        Schaumburg, Illinois

Design

Mires Design's old letterhead didn't emphasize the company name and let the logo carry the design. The new design incorporates the company name into the central design.

2 3 4 5 K e t t n e r B l v d . S a n D i e g o , C A 9 2 1 0 1 6 1 9 2 3 4 6 6 3 1 M i r e s D e s i g n I n c o r p o r a t e d

Client: **Mires Design**
Design Firm: **Mires Design**
                 San Diego, California

MIRES DESIGN INC
2345 KETTNER BLVD SAN DIEGO CA 92101
PHONE: 619 234 6631 FAX: 619 234 1807

CORRESPOND
25 COTTON

ReDesign

Sbemco's old letterhead lacked character and used nondescript colors. The new letterhead uses the company's trademarked blue and pink backing as a basis for corporate identity.

SBEMCO
international, inc.

715 North Finn Drive • Algona, Iowa 50511 • Phone (515) 295-3902 • FAX (515) 295-9545

Client: Sbemco International
Design Firm: Sayles Graphic Design
                  Des Moines, Iowa

INTERNATIONAL, INC.
715 NORTH FINN DRIVE ALGONA, IOWA 50511

CUSTOM SAFETY
FLOOR MATTING

TEL.   (515)295-3902
         (800)468-0860
FAX: (515)295-9545

Index